Express.js

I0011144

Node.js Framework for Web

Application Deveopment

Daniel Green

Disclaimer

While all attempts have been made to verify the information provided in this book, the author doesn't assume any responsibility for errors, omissions, or contrary interpretations of the subject matter contained within. **The information provided in this book is for educational and entertainment purposes only. The reader is responsible for his or her own actions and the author does not accept any responsibilities for any liabilities or damages, real or perceived, resulting from the use of this information.**

The trademarks that are used are without any consent, and the publication of the trademark is without permission or backing by the trademark owner. All trademarks and brands within this book are for clarifying purposes only and are the owned by the owners themselves, not affiliated with this document.

Contents

Book Description

This book is an exploration of the Express js framework. It begins by explaining more about the framework, what it used for, how it is used, and its relation with the Node.js platform. An explanation of the unique features of the framework has also been given in this section. The book then covers how to set up the environment for the Express js. This includes installation of the framework by use of *"npm."*

The guidance includes creation of the directory, making it your working directory, and then the installation of the framework. Requests and response in Express is also discussed. The methods which are related to both the request and the response object are explored in detail. Routing in Express js is then examined. The book will guide you on how to perform basic middleware routing.

You will also learn how to access the parameters that you need in routing. This chapter helps you to properly handle HTTP requests. The book also explains how to create a server which will enable you to send emails.. You will also learn how to upload files of any type from the client to the server. The book guides you on how to handle static files. Management of cookies is discussed in detail, and the book contains instructions on how to use Express so as to render your HTML files.

The following topics are explored:

- Definition

- Installation of Express

- Request and Response

- Routing

- Sending e-mails in Express

- Uploading files in Express

- Serving Static files

- Management of Cookies

- Rendering of an HTML file

- Designing the Front end

- The express-simple-cdn

Introduction

Express js is closely related to Node.js, and it is solely based on the latter. Most of the codes used in the two platforms are almost the same. Those who are familiar with the Node.js framework will find it easy for them to read and understand this book. However, even for beginners, this book is easy to read and understand. This is also how the platform express js is. The framework makes it easy for developers to create an MVC structure for their apps, whether web or mobile, and especially on the server side.

Chapter 1:

Definition

This is a framework which helps developers in the development of web and mobile apps. The framework is based on Node.js. It has several features which assists developers in the development of apps. The framework has the following unique features:

- Allows for setting up of middleware which will provide a response to the HTTP Requests.

- Definition of a routing table which is used for performance of different actions depending on the URL and the HTTP method.

- Provides a dynamic rendering of HTML pages, depending on the arguments which have been passed to the templates.

Express js is the web framework for Node.js. The framework is very lightweight and with it, one can organize the server side of his or her application into the MVC architecture, that is, Model, View, and Controller. This means that you have the choice of using any of the languages on the template part of your application. You also have the choice of using any of the available databases, such as the MongoDB with Mongoose. These will provide the model of the backend part of the application.

With Express js, everything in your application can be well organized, including the views, requests, and routes. When it comes to a routing purpose, then this framework is the best.

With it, all the middleware which is supported by connect will also be made available.

Chapter 2:

Installation of Express

Note that Express js is based on Node js. This means that before installing Express on your system, you must have installed the Node js. We need to be able to use the node terminal so as to create a web application. To do this, we should use "*npm*" so as to install the framework globally. To do this, just run the following command:

npm install express –save

Let us now follow the procedure in detail:

1. Begin by creating a directory which will hold your application, and then make it your working directory. This is shown below:

```
sh-4.3$ mkdir mydirectory
```

Now that we have created the directory, let us make it the working directory:

```
sh-4.3$ cd mydirectory
```

2. We now need to create the package.json file for the application. In this case, we will use the "*npm init*" command as shown below:

```
sh-4.3$ npm init
```

You will be asked to provide a number of details after executing the above command. These include the name and the version for the application. However, you just have to provide the defaults by hitting the "*Return*" key.

3. We now need to install the Express in the directory we just created, and then save it to the list of dependencies that we have. This can be done by executing the following command:

```
$ npm install express --save
```

4. However, it is possible that you may need to temporarily install Express, and not to save it in the list of dependencies that you have. If this is the case, then leave out the option "—save." This is shown below:

```
$ npm install express
```

Note that with the "*npm*" command, the Express will be saved in the directory "*node_modules.*" Note that the installation will be a temporary one. Hower, there are some other modules that need to be installed together with Express. These include the following:

- Body-parser- this is the middleware for Node.js, and it is responsible for handling Raw, JSON, URL, and Text encoded form data. It can be installed as follows:

```
$ npm install body-parser --save
```

- Cookie-parser- this is for paring the cookie header and populating the req.cookies with an object which has been keyed by the names of the cookie. This can be installed as follows:

```
$ npm install cookie-parser --save
```

- Multer- this is just a middleware for Node.js, which is responsible for the handling of multipart/form-data. This can be installed by use of the following command:

```
$ npm install multer --save
```

Hello Application

We need to test our installation by creating a simple *"Hello there!"* application. The application will work by starting the server, and then listen on port number 3000 for a connection. Requests which come from the homepage will be responded to by a *"Hello there!"* message. In case of any other path, then the application will respond with the message "404 Not Found." The example is given below:

```
var ex = require('express');

var application = express();

application.get('/', function (request, response) {

response.send('Hello there!');

})

var server = application.listen(8081, function () {

var host = server.address().address

var port = server.address().port
```

```
console.log("The application is listening at
http://%s:%s", host, port)

})
```

Once you have written the above code, save the file with the

name *"test.js."* Use the following command on the terminal so

as to execute it:

node test.js

The program will give you the following output:

```
The application is listening at http://0.0.0.0:8081
```

Now that it is listening to any connection at port 8081, just

open your browser, and then type the following URL:

http://127.0.0.1:8081/

Once you type the above URL, just hit the *"Return"* key. You

will observe the following output on your browser:

```
Hello there!
```

This shows that our application is working effectively.

Chapter 3:

Request and Response

In Express js, there is the use of the callback functions which make use of both the request and response as the parameters. The following syntax is used:

application.get('/', function (request, response) {

// --

})

The Request Object

This refers to the HTTP request. Some of its properties include the request query string, the body, the parameters, and others.

The following are the other properties which are associated with the request object:

1. Req.app- this is used for holding the Express application instance which uses the middleware part.

2. Req.baseUrl- this is the URL path on which mounting of the instance of the router was mounted.

3. Req.body- this has the key-value pairs of the data which was submitted in the request body. This is not defined by default. Population of this is done after body-passing middle-ware is done.

4. Req.cookies- this is just an object which has cookies which have been sent by the request when using the cookie-parser middleware.

5. Req.fresh- states whether or not the request is fresh.

6. Req.ip- this represents the remote IP address of the request.

7. Req.path- this represents the path part of our request URL.

Methods for the Request Object

The following are some of these methods:

<u>req.accepts(types)</u>

The method is responsible for checking on whether the content types that you have specified are acceptable. This is based on the Accept HTTP header field of the request. Consider the examples given below:

```
// Accept: text/*, application/json
req.accepts('html');
// => "html"
// Accept: text/html
req.accepts('html');
// => "html"
req.accepts('text/html');
// => "text/html"
```

req.get(field)

This method will return the HTTP request header field which has been specified. Consider the example given below:

```
req.get('content-type');
// => "text/plain"
```

req.get('Content-Type');

// => "text/plain"

req.get('Something');

// => undefined

<u>req.is(type)</u>

When the "Content-Type" HTTP header field of the incoming request matches the MIME type which is specified by the type parameter, then this method will return *"true."* Consider the example given below:

// With Content-Type: text/html; charset=utf-8

req.is('html');

req.is('text/html');

req.is('text/*');

// => true

<u>req.param(name [, defaultValue])</u>

With this method, if a parameter is present, then its value will be returned. Consider the following example:

```
// ?name=john

req.param('name')

// => "john"

// POST name=john

req.param('name')

// => "john"

// /user/john for /user/:name

req.param('name')

// => "john"
```

Methods for the Response Object

The object "*res*" in Express is used to represent the response that will be sent by the Express application after receiving an HTTP request.

The object is associated with the following properties:

1. Res.app- this method is used to reference the Express application instance which uses the middleware.

2. Res.headerSent- this is a Boolean property which tells whether or not the application had sent HTTP headers for the response.

3. Res.locals- this is an object which has the local variables for the response which has been scoped with the request.

Response Object Methods

res.append(field [, value])

With this method, the value which you specify is appended to the header field of the HTTP response. Consider the examples given below:

res.append('Link', ['<http://localhost/>', '<http://localhost:4000/>']);

res.append('Set-Cookie', 'foo=bar; Path=/; Http');

res.append('Warning', 'This is a warning');

res.attachment([filename])

While sending an HTTP response, we use this method so as to send attachments. Consider the example given below:

res.attachment('path/to/picture.png');

In the above example, we are attaching a file named *"picture"* and it is a png file.

res.cookie(name, value [, options])

We use this method for setting a cookie name to a value. The parameter value can either be an object or a string which has been converted into JSON.

Consider the example given below:

res.cookie('name', 'john', { domain: '.url.com', path: '/user', secure: true });

res.cookie('box', { items: [a,b,c] });

res.cookie('box', { items: [a,b,c] }, { maxAge: 800000 });

res.clearCookie(name [, options])

In this case, you specify the name of the cookie which is to be cleared. Consider the examples given below:

res.cookie('name', 'john', { path: '/user' });

res.clearCookie('name', { path: '/user' });

res.download(path [, filename] [, fn])

The file which is contained at *"path"* is transferred as an attachment. Under normal circumstances, the user will be prompted to accept the download. An example of this is given below:

```
res.download('/file1.pdf');

res.download('/file2.pdf', 'report.pdf');

res.download('/file3.pdf', 'report.pdf',
function(error){

});
```

res.format(object)

If you need to perform some content negotiation on the header of Accept HTTP on the request object, but when it is present. Consider the examples given below:

```
res.format({

'text/plain': function(){

res.send('Hello');

},

'text/html': function(){

res.send('Hello');
```

```
    },

    'application/json': function(){

    res.send({ message: 'Hello' });

    },


    'default': function() {

    // logging the request and response with 406

    res.status(406).send('Not Allowed');

    }

});
```

Chapter 4:

Routing

With routing in Express js, we are able to determine how our server will respond to client requests at a particular endpoint, which in this case is the path or the URI and an HTTP request method which is specific such as the GRET, POST, and others.

The router is a class in Express which enables us to develop router handlers. This means that our application will not be able to handle routing only, but it will be in a position to handle other issues such as validation, 404, and other types of errors.

The following code is for *"Package.json"*:

```json
{
  "name": "expressRouter",
  "version": "0.0.1",
  "scripts": {
    "start": "node Server.js"
  },
  "dependencies": {
    "express": "^4.12.3"
  }
}
```

Add the above code in a certain file, and then save it. You can then use the following command so as to install the dependencies for Express:

npm install

The following should be the code for the server file "*Server.js*":

```
var exp = require("express");

var app = express();

//Create the Router() object

var router = express.Router();

// Providing all the routes here for the Home page.

router.get("/",function(req,res){

  res.json({"message" : "Hello there!"});

});

// Telling express to use the router with  the /api
before.

// You can use the '/' if any sub path is not needed
before routes.

app.use("/api",router);

// Listening to the Port

app.listen(3000,function(){

 console.log("Listening at Port 3000");

});
```

Just save the file, and then run it by executing the following command:

npm start

The above command will internally trigger the *"node Server.js."* The following message will be observed on the terminal after running the command:

Listening at Port 3000

If you have any Rest simulator on your system, such as the PostMan, just open it, and then navigate to the following URL:

http://localhost:3000/api/

The following message will be printed on the screen:

```
{

"message" : "Hello there!"

}
```

Note that this is the message we have in one of the files.

Basic middleware routing

Note that before the routes are invoked, the middleware will first be executed. This practice has several uses, such as when we want to log every request before we invoke it. We can also use this to determine whether or not a request is proper.

Suppose that we want to determine the kind of a request and then print it, that is, whether GET, POST, or others. Our server file should be as follows:

var exp = require("express");

```
var app = express();

//Create the Router() object

var router = exp.Router();

// Router middleware, we had mentioned it before
the definition of the //routes.

router.use(function(req,res,next) {

  console.log("/" + req.method);

  next();

});

// Providing all the routes here for the Home page.

router.get("/",function(req,res){

  res.json({"message" : "Hello there!"});

});

// Telling express to use the router with the /api
before.

// You canuse '/' if any sub path is not needed before
the routes.

app.use("/api",router);

// Listen to the Port
```

```
app.listen(3000,function(){

  console.log("Listening at Port 3000");

});
```

Just run this app at this point. The following output will be observed at the terminal:

Listening at Port 3000

The purpose of the function "*next()*" is to take the router to the next routes.

How to access parameters in Routing

Routes which contain parameters look as follows:

Route : **http://sample.com/api/:name/**

Route with data : **http://sample.com/api/john/**

We have used the name *"John"* in the above example. These parameters can be accessed on either the Middleware or on the Route.

Accessing parameters in the middleware

Suppose that the parameter has the name *"age."* This is shown in the code given below:

```
// The middle-ware will obtain the age parameter
// checking whether its 0 else move to the next router.
router.use("/user/:age",function(req,res,next){
  if(req.params.age == 0) {
    res.json({"message" : "Age other than 0 must be passed."});
  }
  else next();
});
```

Accessing parameters in Router

To access the parameters that you need in the router, use the following code:

```
router.get("/user/:age",function(req,res){
  res.json({"message" : "Hello "+req.params.age});
});
```

The complete code should be as follows:

```
var exp = require("express");

var app = express();

//Create the Router() object

var router = exp.Router();

// The router middleware, which we mentioned
before defining the routes.

router.use(function(req,res,next) {

  console.log("/" + req.method);
```

```
  next();

});

router.use("/user/:age",function(req,res,next){

  console.log(req.params.age)

  if(req.params.age == 0) {

    res.json({"message" : "Age other than 0 must be
passed."});     }

  else next();

});

// Providing all of the routes for the Home page.

router.get("/",function(req,res){

  res.json({"message" : "Hello there!"});

});

router.get("/user/:id",function(req,res){

  res.json({"message" : "Hello "+req.params.age});

});

// Telling express to use the router with the /api
before.
```

// '/' can be put if any sub path is not needed before routes.

app.use("/api",router);

// Listening to this Port

app.listen(3000,function(){

  console.log("Listening at Port 3000");

});

Run the above code, and then open the browser, and navigate to the following URL:

http://localhost:3000/api/user/john

You can then replace the user *"john"* with 0, and observe the output on the screen. It will be as follows:

```
{
"message" : "Hello there!"
}
```

After passing the 0, you will observe the following error:

```
{

"message" : "Age other than 0 must be passed."

}
```

How to handle 404 errors

When we do not find anything for a particular route, then the return is a 404 error. To handle this, a single middleware is needed together with the route which is to be executed in case none of the available ones are met. The following code can be used for that purpose:

```
var exp = require("express");

var app = express();

//Create a Router() object

var router = exp.Router();
```

```
// Router middleware, which we mentioned before
definition of the routes.

router.use(function(req,res,next) {

  console.log("/" + req.method);

  next();

});

router.use("/user/:age",function(req,res,next){

  console.log(req.params.age)

  if(req.params.age == 0) {

    res.json({"message" : "Age other than 0 must be
passed"});

  }

  else next();

});

// all the routes will be provided here, and they are
for the Home page.

router.get("/",function(req,res){

  res.json({"message" : "Hello there!"});

});
```

```
router.get("/user/:age",function(req,res){

  res.json({"message" : "Hello "+req.params.age});

});

// Handling the 404 error.

// This is the last middleware.

app.use("*",function(req,res){

  res.status(404).send('404');

});

// Telling express to make use of the router with the
/api before.

// '/' can be put if any sub path is not needed before
the routes.

app.use("/api",router);

// Listening to the Port

app.listen(3000,function(){

  console.log("Listening at Port 3000");

});
```

You can then run the above code. You can also try to hit different routes. You should get the following output on the screen:

404

Application's sample routes

Consider the following code for "*server.js*":

```
var exp = require("express");

var app = express();

var router = express.Router();

router.use(function (req,res,next) {

  console.log("/" + req.method);

  next();

});

router.use("/user/:age",function(req,res,next){
```

```
  console.log(req.params.age)

 if(req.params.age == 0) {

  res.json({"message" : "Age other than 0 must be
passed."});

 }

 else next();

});

router.get("/",function(req,res){

 res.sendFile(__dirname + "/public/index.html");

});

router.get("/about",function(req,res){

 res.sendFile(__dirname + "/public/about.html");

});

router.get("/user/:age",function(req,res){

 res.json({"message" : "Hello "+req.params.age});

});

app.use("/",router);

app.use("*",function(req,res){
```

```
    res.sendFile(__dirname + "/public/404.html");

});

app.listen(3000,function(){

    console.log("Listening at Port 3000");

});
```

You can then run the above program, and then visit the home page. The home page in this case is the "/" and the "/*about.*" The 404 error response on one's browser should be as follows:

404 !

By the use of the Express router, the routing capability of one's app can be extended. You will be in a position to organize the routes and use multiple behavior for a particular route.

However, this will depend on the HTTP method which has been used.

In one of our previous examples, you learned how to respond to client requests for the homepage. We now want to extend this program. This is given below:

```
var exp = require('express');

var app = express();

// The response for this will be "Hello there!" on the homepage

app.get('/', function (req, res) {

console.log("Obtained a GET request for our homepage");

res.send('Hey GET method');

})

// This will respond a POST request for our homepage

app.post('/', function (req, res) {
```

```
console.log("Obtained a POST request for our
homepage");

res.send('Hey POST');

})

// This will respond a DELETE request for our
/remove_user page.

app.delete('/remove_user', function (req, res) {

console.log("Obtained a DELETE request for the
/remove_user");

res.send('Hey DELETE');

})

// This will respond a GET request for our
/show_user page.

app.get('/show_user', function (req, res) {

console.log("Obtained a GET request for  the
/show_user");

res.send('Listing the page');

})

// This will respond a GET request for wxyz, wxayz,
wx123yz, and so on

app.get('/wx*yz', function(req, res) {
```

```
console.log("Obtained a GET request for /wx*yz");

res.send('The Page Pattern was Matched');

})

var server = app.listen(8081, function () {

var host = server.address().address

var port = server.address().port

console.log("The app is listening at http://%s:%s",
host, port)

})
```

Just write the above code, and then save it with the name
"*test.js,*" Run it by opening the terminal, and running the
following command:

node test.js

Once you execute the above command, you will observe the
following output:

```
The app is listening at http://0.0.0.0:8081
```

This shows that our server is ready, and that it is waiting for the client to send the requests. Let us try to send different requests to the server *"server.js"* and observe the kind of response that we get. These are shown below:

The following screenshot shows the page for *"show_user"*:

Listing the page

Be focused on the URL. We have used this to navigate to the page.

Consider the screenshot shown below:

The Page Pattern was Matched

The text which we specified for the page has been displayed. Notice that in the above example screenshots, we have tried to obtain the pages which we have created. What if we try to obtain one which we did not create? Consider the screenshot shown below:

Cannot GET/stuv

As shown in the screenshot, we are trying to get the page "*stuv*" which is not available. You can see the kind of response that we got from the server "*server.js.*"

Chapter 5:

Sending e-mails in Express

We need to use the Express js and the NodeMailer so as to send e-mails to our recipients. By the end of this tutorial, you will have created an Express application with the ability to send emails to other accounts. Follow the steps given below:

Create a new file, and give it the name *"package.json."* Add the following code to the file:

```
{
"name": "email-node",
"version": "1.0.0",
"dependencies": {
```

```
"nodemailer": "~0.7.1",

"express": "~4.5.1"

}

}
```

Save the file in the folder of choice. Once the file is ready, open the command prompt or the terminal, and then navigate to the folder. Once you are there, type the following command:

npm install

With the above command, all the dependencies which our project needs will be downloaded. Once completed, you will be in a position to see a folder named *"node_modules"* in the directory for your project.

Implementation of the Server.js

Create a new file, and then give it the name *"server.js."* Add the following code to the file:

```
var exp =require('express');

var nmailer = require("nodemailer");

var app=express();

app.listen(3000,function(){

console.log("Express was started on the Port 3000");

});
```

The above codes are the basics for our application. Running it on the terminal will print a message. We now want to instruct it on how to react in case a request is sent from the browser. This can be done by adding some routing logic to our app.

Identify the line *"app.listen"* and then add the following code just above it:

```
app.get('/',function(req,res){

res.sendfile('index.html');

});
```

At this time, if the app is run on the browser, then the content of the file "*index.html*" will be printed. Some part of the file should be as follows:

```
<div id="container">

<div></div>

Express.JS Email application

<div>

<h1>The Mailer</h1>

<input id="to" type="text" placeholder="Enter the email of the recipient" />

<input id="subject" type="text" placeholder="Add Subject" />

<textarea id="content" cols="40" rows="5" placeholder=You're your message here"></textarea>

<button id="send ">Send Email</button>

<span id="message"></span>
```

</div>

The above HTML code should present yourself with the
following interface:

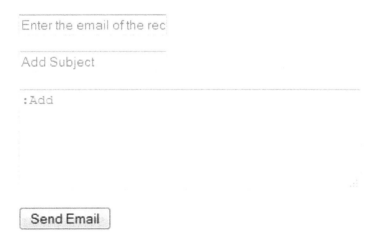

Express.JS Email application

The Mailer

Now that our server is ready and that we have the interface, we
need to come up with a mechanism on how to call the server

once the *"Send Email"* button has been pressed. We need to do this at the side of the client, meaning that we have to use some JQuery. The code for this is given below:

```
<script>
$(document).ready(function(){

    var from, to, subject, message;

    $("#send ").click(function(){

        to=$("#to").val();

        subject=$("#subject").val();

        message=$("#content").val();

        $("#message").text("The email is being sent,
please wait...");


$.get("http://localhost:3000/send",{to:to,subject:subject,message:text},function(d){

        if(d=="sent")

        {

            $("#message").empty().html("
```

The Email will be sent at "+to+" . Kindly check the inbox !

");

}

});

});

});

</script>

We now need to add a router in the file *"Server.js"* and this will deal with our requests. Note that these are the route requests. In the file *"Server.js,"* identify the line "app.get('/')" and then add the following code just below it:

app.get('/send',function(req,res){

//code for sending the e-mail.

//Will be available soon.

});

Adding code for the NodeMailer

Our intention at this point is to handle the mail system. We should start by defining the Mail Transport System (SMTP), so that we can be able to send an email from our email box. If you need to ensure a high level of security, then you can choose to add your Gmail account together with your password.

Open the file *"Server.js"* and identify the line "var app=express()." Add the following code just below this line:

var sTransport = nmailer.createTransport("SMTP",{

service: "Gmail",

auth: {

user: "email@gmail.com",

pass: "Add the Gmail password"

}

});

This is the object which is to be used for sending the email. Our intention is that after the user clicks on the button labeled *"Send Email,"* the email will be directly sent. This part of the app has already been accomplished. In the block **"app.get('/send')"**, add the following code:

```
var mOptions={

to : req.query.to,

subject : req.query.subject,

text : req.query.text

}

console.log(mOptions);

sTransport.sendMail(mOptions, function(err, response){

if(err){

console.log(err);

res.end("err");

}else{
```

```
console.log("The Message has been sent: " +
response.message);

res.end("sent");

}

});
```

What we have done in the above code is that the GET variables which have been sent from the HTML page have been read. We have then used the Transport function which we had created to call our *"sendEmail()"* function. However, I understand that most of you might be confused by this. To avoid this, find the complete *"Server.js"* file below:

```
var exp =require('express');

var nmailer = require("nodemailer");

var app=express();

/*
```

Configuring the details of our server.

We have used SMTP for this purpose, which is a mail server responsible for sending and response of emails.
*/

```javascript
var sTransport = nmailer.createTransport("SMTP",{

service: "Gmail",

auth: {

user: "name@gmail.com",

pass: "Add the G-mail password"

}

});
/*----------------SMTP Over---------------------------*/

/*----------------Routing Started ---------------------*/

app.get('/',function(req,res){

res.sendfile('index.html');

});

app.get('/send',function(req,res){
```

```javascript
var mOptions={

to : req.query.to,

subject : req.query.subject,

text : req.query.message

}

console.log(mOptions);

sTransport.sendMail(mOptions, function(err, response){

if(err){

console.log(err);

res.end("err");

}else{

console.log("The Message has been sent: " + response.message);

res.end("sent");

}

});

});
```

```
/*-------------------Routing Over--------------------------*/

app.listen(3000,function(){

console.log("Express was started on the Port 3000");

});
```

Our HTML page with all the JS and the styles should be as follows:

```
<html>

<head>

<title>Express Email application</title>

<script
src="//ajax.googleapis.com/ajax/libs/jquery/1.11.1/jq
uery.min.js"></script><script>// <![CDATA[

$(document).ready(function(){

   var from,to,subject,message;

   $("#send ").click(function(){

      to=$("#to").val();

      subject=$("#subject").val();
```

```
text=$("#content").val();

    $("#message").text("The email is being sent.
Please wait...");

    $.get("http://localhost:3000/send",{to: to,
subject: subject, message: text},function(d){

    if(d =="sent")

    {

        $("#message").empty().html("

The Email has been sent at "+to+" . Kindly check your
inbox !

");

    }

});

    });

});

</script>

</head>

<body>

<div id="container">
```

```html
<h1>Mailer In Express.JS</h1>

<input id="to" type="text" placeholder="Enter the E-mail of the recipient" />

<input id="subject" type="text" placeholder="Add Subject" />

<textarea id="content" cols="40" rows="5" placeholder=You're your message here"></textarea>

<button id="send ">Send Email</button>

<span id="message"></span>

</div>

</div>
```

At this point, your application is fully working, so just run it and observe the result that you get. For the first time, you will be presented with the user interface where you can enter the details of the Email including the recipient, the subject, and the message itself. This is shown below:

Express.JS Email application

The Mailer

Enter the email of the rec

Add Subject

: Add

Send Email

Just enter the respective details, and then hit the "*Send Email*"

button. The email will be sent.

Chapter 6:

Uploading files in Express

In this chapter, we will use the Express framework and the *"multer"* middleware for the purpose of uploading files. The middleware was developed for the purpose of handling form/multi-part data.

The form *"target"* parameter will be set to the router.

The project

We will start be designing an Express server. This will be responsible for handling the task of routing and some other stuff. Multer will be responsible for handling the file uploads, and the HTML part will handle the input to the form.

Create a new file and give it the name *"Package.json."* It should have the following code:

```
{
  "name": "file_upload",
  "version": "0.0.1",
  "dependencies": {
    "express": "~4.10.2",
    "multer": "~0.1.6"
  }
}
```

We now need to install the dependency. The above package should have been saved in a particular folder. Open the terminal or the command prompt, and then navigate to that folder. Type the following command:

npm install

This will install the stuff which is required.

The file *"Server.js"* should have the following code:

```
/*Defining the dependencies.*/

var exp=require("express");

var multer  = require('multer');

var app=express();

var success = false;

/*Configuring the multer.*/

app.use(multer({ dest: './files/',

rename: function (fdname, filename) {

   return filename+Date.now();

 },

onFileUploadStart: function (myfile) {

   console.log(myfile.originalname + ' is being started ...')
```

```
	},

	onFileUploadComplete: function (myfile) {

		console.log(myfile.fdname + ' uploaded to  ' +
		myfile.path)

		success=true;

	}

}));

/*Handling the routes.*/

app.get('/',function(req,res){

	res.sendfile("index.html");

});

app.post('/api/photo',function(req,res){

	if(success==true){

		console.log(req.files);

		res.end("File was successfully uploaded.");

	}

});

/*Running the server.*/
```

```
app.listen(3000,function(){

  console.log("Work being done on port 3000");

});
```

We need the form which is to be used for uploading the file by providing us with the interface. Its code will be given soon. Create a new file, and then give it the name "*Index.html.*" The following should be the code for the file:

```
<form id =  "FileUpload"
   enctype  = "multipart/form-data"
   action  = "/api/photo"
   method  = "post"
>
<input type="file" name="photo" />
<input type="submit" value="Upload your Image" name="submit">
</form>
```

The above code provides a form similar to the following:

Browse_   No file selected.

Upload your Image

We want you to browse for the image after clicking on the "*Browse*" button. The image should be uploaded to the server once you click on the "*Upload your Image*" button.

The project is now ready, meaning that you can run it. Just copy all of the files into a single folder. Open the terminal or the command prompt, and then navigate to that folder. Just type the following command:

node server.js

With the above command, the project will be run. The server is now up and running. Navigate to the "*localhost:3000.*" You will be in a position to view the app. Just select your file, and then check the folder named *"files."* You will find your file there.

Explanation

What we have done is that we have configured the multer in the file *"sserver.js."* The purpose of the multer is to emit events at particular circumstances. Once you start to upload your file, the event *"onFileUpload"* will be emitted.

Once the upload is done, the variable for *"myfile"* will hold the following information in an array:

```
{
  photo:
   {
     fieldname: 'photo',
     originalname: 'john.png',
     name: 'john1515879449314.png',
```

```
    encoding: '7bit',

    mimetype: 'image/png',

    path: 'files\\ john1515879449314.png ',

    extension: 'png',

    size: 11600,

    truncated: false,

    buffer: null

  }

}
```

The information shown above contains the details which describe the file.

For the sake of passing the names of our files, we have used the *"rename"* but by default, the multer will use the default names for uniqueness.

Notice that we are emitting the *"onFileUploadComplete"* event. It is after this that we have set the variable *"success."*

This event will tell us whether or not the file was uploaded successfully. This code is shown below:

```
if(success==true){
   console.log(req.files);
   res.end("File was successfully uploaded.");
}
```

Note the use of the "enctype="multipart/form-data"" in the HTML. If this is not mentioned, then our multer will not work.

It is also possible for us to use the multer so as to validate the file on the server end. It provides us with the *"limits"* array parameter which provides us with the following parameters:

- fieldSize- this is the maximum size of the field. It is an integer with a default value of 1MB.

- fieldNameSize- the maximum size of the name field. It is an integer with a default value of 100 bytes.

- fileSize- this is the maximum size of the file in multipart forms. It is an integer measured in bytes.

- Files- this is the maximum number of file fields for the multipart forms. It is an integer that can take an infinite size.

- headerPairs- this is an integer which takes a maximum size of 2000. It represents the maximum number of header keys for the multipart forms.

To define these, use the syntax given below:

limits: {

  fieldNameSize: 50,

  files: 4,

  fields: 5

}

For our code, we should have the following:

```
app.use(multer({ dest: './files/',

 rename: function (fdname, filename) {

   return filename+Date.now();

 },

limits: {

 fieldNameSize: 50,

 files: 4,

 fields: 4

}

}));
```

You have now seen the importance of the multer. The Express

community is responsible for the development of the multer.

Chapter 7:

Serving Static files

In Express js, there is a file named *"express.static"* which can help in the serving of static files. These files include the CSS, images, and the JavaScript. What happens is that you have to pass the path where the static files are located to the *"express.static"* middleware so that it can start the process of directly serving the files.

Suppose that you have kept your files in a directory named *"users,"* and then you can do the following:

app.use(express.static('users'));

Suppose that we have the sub-directory *"users/image,"* we can keep a few of the images as follows:

node_modules

server.js

users/

users/images

users/images/picture.png

Remember the *"Hello there!"* app which we created earlier. We need to modify it so that it can be able to handle static files. Consider the code given below:

```
var exp = require('express');

var app = express();

app.use(exp.static('users'));
```

```
app.get('/', function (req, res) {

res.send('Hello there!');

})

var server = app.listen(8081, function () {

var host = server.address().address

var port = server.address().port

console.log("The sample app is listening at
http://%s:%s", host, port)

})
```

The file should act as the server, so give it the name *"server.js"*

and then save it. You can then open your browser and then

navigate to the following URL:

http://127.0.0.1:8081/images/picture.png

You will observe the following on the browser:

If you specified a different image compared to the one I have used, then the output will be of a different image.

The GET method

We are going to give an example which uses the Form GET method in HTML so as to pass two values. The input will be handled by the router *"process_get"* inside the file *"server.js."* The code is given below:

<html>

```html
<body>

<form action="http://127.0.0.1:8081/process_get"
method="GET">

Your First Name: <input type="text" name="fname">
<br>

Your Last Name: <input type="text" name="lname">

<input type="submit" value="Submit">

</form>

</body>

</html>
```

Just write the above code, and then save the file with the name
"*index.html.*" The next step is to add some modifications to the
file "*server.js*" so as to handle the requests from the home
page, and the input which is received from our HTML form.
The code should be as follows:

```js
var exp = require('express');

var app = express();
```

```
app.use(exp.static('users'));

app.get('/index.htm', function (req, res) {

res.sendFile( __dirname + "/" + "index.htm" );

})

app.get('/process_get', function (req, res) {

// Preparing the output in JSON format

response = {

fname:req.query.fname,

lname:req.query.lname

};

console.log(response);

res.end(JSON.stringify(response));

})

var server = app.listen(8081, function () {

var host = server.address().address

var port = server.address().port

console.log("The sample app is listening at
http://%s:%s", host, port)
```

})

Now you can open your browser, and then browse to the following:

http://127.0.0.1:8081/index.html

The above will display the following output on your browser:

Your First Name:
Your Last Name:
Submit

The above shows the HTML form which we just created in the HTML file. Just provide the details, that is, the first and the last names, and then hit the *"Submit"* button. You will observe the following output:

{"fname":"John","lname":"George"}

The POST method

We want to give an example which uses the HTML POST method so as to pass two values. We will use the router "*process_get*" inside our file "*server.js.*" The code is given below:

```html
<html>

<body>

<form action="http://127.0.0.1:8081/process_post" method="POST">

Your First Name: <input type="text" name="fname">
<br>

Your Last Name: <input type="text" name="lname">

<input type="submit" value="Submit">

</form>

</body>

</html>
```

The above code should be saved in a file with the name "*index.html.*" The file "*serve.js*" should be modified so as to handle the requests which come from the home page, and the input received from the HTML form. The code for this is given below:

```
var exp = require('express');

var app = express();

var bParser = require('body-parser');

// Creating the application/x-www-form-urlencoded parser

var urlenParser = bParser.urlencoded({ extended: false })

app.use(exp.static('users'));

app.get('/index.htm', function (req, res) {

res.sendFile( __dirname + "/" + "index.htm" );

})

app.post('/process_post', urlenParser, function (req, res) {
```

```
// Preparing the output in JSON format

response = {

fname:req.body.fname,

lname:req.body.lname

};

console.log(response);

res.end(JSON.stringify(response));

})

var server = app.listen(8081, function () {

var host = server.address().address

var port = server.address().port

console.log("The sample application is listening at
http://%s:%s", host, port)

})
```

You can then open the browser, and then navigate to the

following URL:

http://127.0.0.1:8081/index.htm

The above URL will direct you to the following page:

Your First Name: _____

Your Last Name: _____

[Submit]

This is the HTML form that we created. Just provide the details which are needed as shown in the form. Once done, just hit the *"Submit"* button. The following will be observed:

{"fname":"John","lname":"George"}

Chapter 8:

Management of Cookies

In Express js, it is possible for us to send some cookies to the Node.js server. This server will then use a middleware so as to handle the cookies. We now need to come up with an example in which the server will print the cookies which are sent to it by the client. The code is given below:

```
var exp = require('express')

var cParser = require('cookie-parser')

var app = express()

app.use(cParser())

app.get('/', function(req, res) {

console.log("The cookies are: ", req.cookies)
```

```
})
```

app.listen(8081)

With the above example, the server will listen to port number 8081. This is the port where the client will pass the cookies. The server will then print these cookies. This is how they can be handled in Express js.

Chapter 9:

Rendering of an HTML file

You need to know how you can handle HTML files in Express js. With this framework, it is possible for you to create a custom web server depending on what you need. This means that you can also choose the kind of packages which you can install on your system rather than installing multiple of these. However, if you have Node.js installed on your system, then you are already set.

Express js comes with a method called *"sendFile()"* which can be used to send HTML files to the browser. The browser will then automatically interpret these. Our aim is to deliver the appropriate HTML file to each of the routes. Consider the code given below:

```
//assume the app is an express Object.
app.get('/',function(req,res){
    res.sendFile('index.html');
});
```

The code is just an example. Running it will cause an error.

We need to demonstrate how this can be done. We should create a simple website made up of three pages, that is the Home, About us, and the link to the site page. For the sake of handling the events, we will use jQuery while Bootstrap will be used to design the web pages.

The file *"PACKAGE.json"* should have the following code:

```
{
  "name": "express-html",
  "version": "0.0.1",
  "dependencies": {
```

```
    "express": "^4.11.0"

  }
}
```

Just navigate to the folder having the above via the command line or the terminal. Use the following command, so as to install the dependencies:

npm install

Start the server by running the following command:

node server.js

The following is the code for the express server:

```
var exp = require("express");

var app    = express();

var p    = require("path");

app.get('/',function(req,res){
```

```
res.sendFile(p.join(__dirname+'/index.html'));

//__dirname : this will be resolved to the folder of
the project.

});

app.get('/about',function(req,res){

res.sendFile(path.join(__dirname+'/about.html'));

});

app.get('/sitemap',function(req,res){

res.sendFile(path.join(__dirname+'/sitemap.html'));

});

app.listen(3000);

console.log("Now running at the Port 3000");
```

Our HTML files are as follows:

```
<html>

<head>

  <title>Express and HTML</title>
```

```html
<script
src="https://ajax.googleapis.com/ajax/libs/jquery/1.1
1.2/jquery.min.js"></script>

<link rel="stylesheet"
href="https://maxcdn.bootstrapcdn.com/bootstrap/3
.3.1/css/bootstrap.min.css">

<link rel="stylesheet"
href="https://maxcdn.bootstrapcdn.com/bootstrap/3
.3.1/css/bootstrap-theme.min.css">

<script
src="https://maxcdn.bootstrapcdn.com/bootstrap/3.
3.1/js/bootstrap.min.js"></script>

</head>

<body>

  <div style="margin:100px;">

    <nav class="navbar navbar-inverse navbar-static-
top">

  <div class="container">

    <a class="navbar-brand" href="/">Express
HTML</a>

   <ul class="nav navbar-nav">

     <li class="active">

       <a href="/">Home</a>
```

```html
      </li>

      <li>

        <a href="/about">About us</a>

      </li>

      <li>

        <a href="/sitemap">SiteDirectory</a>

      </li>

    </ul>

  </div>

</nav>

  <div class="jumbotron" style="padding:50px;">

    <h1>Hello, there!</h1>

    <p> Express js comes with a method called
"sendFile()" which can be used to send HTML files to
the browser. The browser will then automatically
interpret these.</p>

    <p><a class="btn btn-primary btn-lg" href="#"
role="button">Explore more...</a></p>

  </div>
```

```
    </div>

  </body>

</html>
```

The above code should give you the following output:

Our aim is to resolve each path contained in each of the routes. We can perform some optimization to this. With the configuration variable which is provided by Express, you can define the static path for the file. This means that there will be no need for us to resolve the path for each of the routes. This can be done as follows:

var exp = require("express");

```javascript
var app    = express();

app.use(exp.static(__dirname + '/View'));

//Storing all of the HTML files in the view folder.

app.use(exp.static(__dirname + '/Script'));

//Storing all of the JS and the CSS in the Scripts
folder.

app.get('/',function(req,res){

  res.sendFile('index.html');

  //This will find and then locate the file index.html
from the View or Scripts

});

app.get('/about',function(req,res){

  res.sendFile('/about.html');

});

app.get('/sitedirectory',function(req,res){

  res.sendFile('/sitedirectory.html');

});

app.listen(3000);
```

console.log("Now running at the Port 3000");

You are now done. In some particular scenarios, you might need to develop a server which will deliver your HTML files in the same way that Apache does. However, with Express.js, this is different. However, it is also possible for you to develop a custom web server for your application.

Chapter 10:

Designing the Front end

The front end is very key for your application. If you develop a very good front end for your app, but you make the front very poor, and then there are high chances that your app will fail to satisfy the needs of the users. Before developing the app, determine the expectations of the potential users of the app in terms of the front end. This will make them e satisfied with it, and your app will succeed.

With Express js, it is possible for the developer to template their web applications including the advanced ones. and this will create satisfaction on the part of the users. The good thing with Express is that a single template can be used for the performance of different and multiple operations. A good example of this is when I create a file having a div ID, a head, and a title which are coming from the server. This can be set as many times as we want, depending on our call to the routes.

How to pass data to the view

Consider the code given below:

```
app.get('/',function(req,res)
        res.render('index',{title:"Home"});
});
```

The example is not working, we have just passed some data to it. Suppose we want to access the variable *"title"* in the above code. The following code for the file *"index.js"* can be used:

```
<html>

<head>

<title><%= title %></title>

</head>

</html>
```

With the method which we have just used, one can easily pass data from the server, and then access it as it has been shown. This is one of the interesting features offered by Express js.

Splitting the code into multiple parts

Most of you are experts either in Rails or PHP, or even both. You are aware that the code can be divided into several files. This feature is supported in Express js. If you need to include those partial files, then use the following piece of code:

```
<% include FILENAME %>
```

An example of this is given below:

```
<html>
  <head>
    <% include('title.ejs') %>
  </head>
  <body>
    <% include('body.ejs') %>
  </body>
</html>
```

The following is the code for the partial file "*title.js*":

```
<title>
Hello there!
</title>
<script src="jquery.js"></script>
<script>
...Add your JavaScript code in this section.
</script>
```

The code for the partial file *"body.ejs"* should be as follows:

```html
<div id="login">

    <input type="TEXT" name="uname"
value=""><br>

    <input type="password" name="password"
value=""><br>

    <input type="button" name="login"
value="Login">

</div>
```

This code should give you the following form:

Username: ⬜
Password: ⬜
[Login]

Filters in Express js

Express js comes with filters which help developers to perform some modifications to their data without having to write any Javascript code. These operations include the following:

- size.

- Capitalize letter.

- sort.

- Downcase letter.

- length.

They are well known for how friendly they are to the users. A sample code is given:

app.all('/file/*', requireAuthentication, loadUser);

```
app.get('/file/view', function(req, res) {

res.render('file_view');

});

app.get('/file/list', function(req, res) {

res.render('file_list');

});
```

Chapter 11:

The express-simple-cdn

This is a Node.js which is used in express js for the purpose of making it easy for developers to use the CDN for their static assets. With this module, multiple CDN hosts are supported for the purpose of distribution of static assets among numerous hosts.

To install this module on your system, just open the terminal or the command prompt, and then run the following command:

npm install express-simple-cdn

We now need to give an example of how this module can be used in one's app. Our assumption is that you are making use of Jade in your application. This should have been added to the "*app.configure*" for your Express, so if you have not done that, just do it. The configurations for the CDN host should also be different, depending on whether you want these to be used in a development or in a production environment.

The CDN module can be called as follows:

var CDN = require('express-simple-cdn');

A template variable assignment should then be added having the host options for the CDN. The specified CDN host will always be used by the configuration. Consider the code given below:

app.locals.CDN = function(path) { return CDN(path, '//mycdn.com') };

// In Jade, the script(src=CDN('/js/myscript.js')) will be written as
script(src='//mycdn.com/js/myscript.js')

Your URLs will be hashed to any of the CDN hosts which have been specified in an array. This is shown below:

```
app.locals.CDN = function(path) { return CDN(path,
['//cdn1.mycdn.com', '//cdn2.mycdn.com',
'//cdn3.mycdn.com']) };
```

// In Jade, the script(src=CDN('/js/myscript.js')) will be written as
script(src='//cdnX.mycdn.com/js/myscript.js'), and X will be a consistent bucket number.

With this configuration, the version number of the file will be shown in the URL, and the CDN network will always be pulling the newer versions of your file once the updates have been pushed, and the *"uFVersion"* has been passed as true. This is shown below:

```
server.locals.CDN = function (path, uFVersion) {

if(uFVersion === undefined || uFVersion == false)

return CDN(path, config.CDNURL);

else
```

```
return CDN(path, config.CDNURL,
config.CDNVersion);

};
```

If you need to use the CDN function in the Jade template, use the following code:

```
// JavaScript

script(src=CDN('/js/myscript.js'))

// CSS

link(href=CDN('/css/mycss.css'), rel='stylesheet')


// Files

img(src=CDN('/image/picture.png'))
```

Conclusion

It can be concluded that Express js is a framework which is solely based on Node.js. Most of its code is related to what we have in the latter platform. The framework was developed to make it easy for developers to create web and mobile apps. With the use of the framework, the developer can easily handle the requests which come from the client by creating a server.

The framework also provides the user with the option of development of a routing table which will tell the user what to do, depending on the HTTP method and the URL which has been provided. The user is also allowed to pass some arguments to the templates. This will specify the kind of a dynamic web page which will be rendered. Most web developers, and especially those developing complex web applications, like to use the express framework.

With this framework, they are able to organize the server-side of their app into the MVC architecture, that is, the Model, the View, and the Controller. This makes it possible for the developers to use any kind of language for development of the template or the user interface part of the app. This shows how the framework makes the work of programming very flexible.

The model, which is mainly the database part of your app, can be made of any type of database. The overall structure of the app will be organized. Before beginning to use the framework for a programming purpose, you need to install it on your machine. However, we said that Express is solely based on Node.js. This means that the latter must be installed before installing the former, otherwise, things will not work correctly.

To install the framework, we use the "*npm*" command. You should begin by creating a directory where the installation will be done. Make it the working directory, and then continue with the installation. After the installation, you can test it and then continue.

www.ingramcontent.com/pod-product-compliance
Lightning Source LLC
Chambersburg PA
CBHW071005050326
40689CB00014B/3493